SKYROCKET YOUR PROFITS

By

Dr. Javnyuy Joybert

SKYROCKET YOUR PROFITS:

30 Marketing & Sales Proven Strategies to Boost Your Sales

Step by Step Implementation Guide

By

Dr. Javnyuy Joybert

By Dr. Javnyuy Joybert

TABLE OF CONTENTS

By Dr. Javnyuy Joybert

INTRODUCTION

*A*s an entrepreneur with a decade of experience starting and running businesses (7), I have seen both success and failure. While three of my ventures have not been as successful as I had hoped, I am proud to say that four are still thriving.

I have always been passionate about marketing and sales, and have put this passion to use in my own businesses as well as in my role as a business trainer and consultant, working with clients in over 20 countries to develop and execute strategies that have resulted in millions of dollars in sales.

In this handbook, I want to share some of the knowledge and insights I have gained through my experiences as an entrepreneur and business trainer. These are ideas that have the potential to make a real impact in your business.

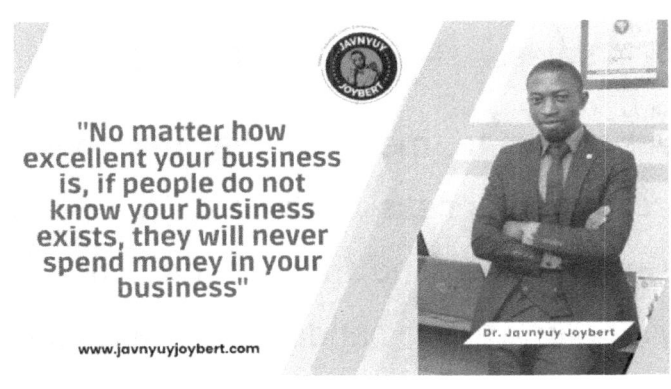

"No matter how excellent your business is, if people do not know your business exists, they will never spend money in your business"

www.javnyuyjoybert.com

Dr. Javnyuy Joybert

I have also seen first-hand the power of access to the right knowledge. In 2021, I posed a question to my business mentorship community: how many of you have been in business for more than two years but have not yet reached the million mark? A few people raised their hands, and I made it my mission to work with them and help them achieve this milestone.

By November 2021, eight of them had already achieved their first million in sales, and the final two reached this goal by December. Some even surpassed this goal, making even more in sales.

It was clear to me that the key to their success was access to the right knowledge and information. And that is what I hope to provide in this handbook - practical, applicable business knowledge that can help you take your business to new heights.

CHAPTER 1

STOP THE CONFUSION: MARKETING IS DIFFERENT FROM SALES

Marketing and sales are often used interchangeably, but they are actually two distinct concepts. Marketing refers to the activities a company undertakes to promote its products or services, such as advertising, public relations, social media, and content creation. The goal of marketing is to create awareness and interest in the company's offerings and to attract potential customers.

On the other hand, sales refers to the process of persuading a potential customer to make a purchase. This includes activities

1

such as making sales presentations, negotiating prices, and closing deals. The goal of sales is to convert potential customers into paying customers.

While marketing and sales are related and often work together, they are distinct activities with different goals and objectives.

Understanding the difference between marketing and sales is important for businesses, as it allows them to develop targeted strategies and allocate resources appropriately.

As an entrepreneur, I always emphasize the importance of understanding the difference between marketing and sales. Marketing is about creating awareness and interest in your business and its offerings, while sales is about persuading potential customers to make a purchase.

But let me ask you, what are you doing to make sure that people know your business exists? When someone comes into contact with your business, are you confident that they will choose to spend their money with you?

In simple terms, marketing is what you do to let people know you exist and that you have something valuable to offer. Sales is what you do to get people to give you their money. It's essential for businesses to have a strong marketing strategy in place to attract potential customers, and to have a sales process

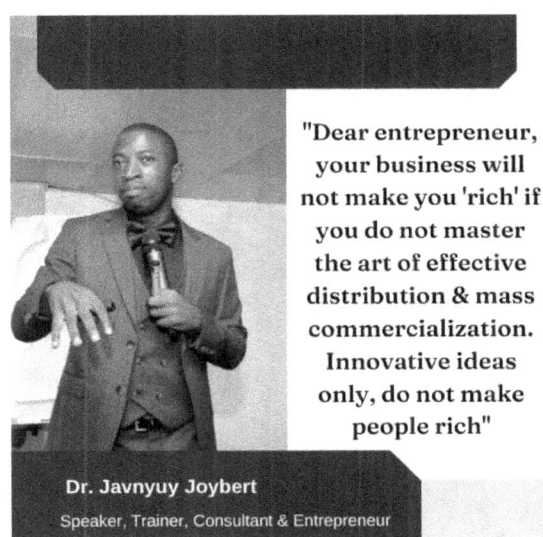

"Dear entrepreneur, your business will not make you 'rich' if you do not master the art of effective distribution & mass commercialization. Innovative ideas only, do not make people rich"

Dr. Javnyuy Joybert
Speaker, Trainer, Consultant & Entrepreneur

in place to convert those potential customers into paying customers.

So, what are you doing to make sure your business stands out and attracts the attention of potential customers?

And once you have their attention, what are you doing to persuade them to make a purchase?

These are important questions to consider as you work to grow and succeed in your business.

CHAPTER 2

FOUNDATION: THE DIFFERENCE AND THE RELATIONSHIP BETWEEN TRADITIONAL & DIGITAL MARKETING

Traditional marketing refers to marketing efforts that use traditional media such as print, radio, television, and outdoor advertising to reach consumers. This can include things like print ads in newspapers and magazines, commercials on radio and television, and billboards and other outdoor advertisements.

Digital marketing, on the other hand, refers to marketing efforts that use digital technologies and platforms to reach consumers. This includes things like social media marketing, email marketing, search engine optimization (SEO), pay-per-click advertising, and mobile app marketing.

Both traditional and digital marketing have their own unique advantages and can be effective in reaching different target audiences. Traditional marketing can be particularly effective for reaching a mass audience, as it allows businesses to reach a large number of people through mediums that have a long reach. Digital marketing, on the other hand, can be more targeted and allows businesses to reach specific demographics or target audiences through the use of data and analytics.

It's important for businesses to consider both traditional and digital marketing when developing their marketing strategies, as the right mix of tactics can be effective in reaching and engaging with potential customers.

Let us break it down further

Both traditional and digital marketing can be effective in reaching and engaging with potential customers, and the right mix of tactics will depend on the specific needs and goals of the business. Here are a few key differences between traditional and digital

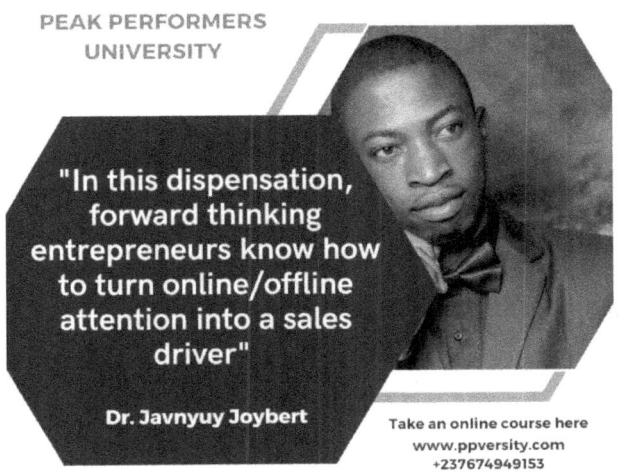

PEAK PERFORMERS
UNIVERSITY

"In this dispensation, forward thinking entrepreneurs know how to turn online/offline attention into a sales driver"

Dr. Javnyuy Joybert

Take an online course here
www.ppversity.com
+237674949153

marketing:

Reach

Traditional marketing typically has a wider reach, as it uses mediums that are accessible to a large number of people. Digital marketing, on the other hand, can be more targeted, as it allows businesses to use data and analytics to reach specific demographics or target audiences.

Cost

Traditional marketing can be more expensive than digital marketing, as it often involves the cost of creating and placing ads in various mediums. Digital marketing can be more cost -effective, as it allows businesses to reach a large audience at a lower cost per impression.

Tracking And Measurement

Digital marketing offers more opportunities for tracking and measurement, as it allows businesses to use analytics and other tools to track the effectiveness of their campaigns and make adjustments as needed. Traditional marketing can be more difficult to track and measure, as it often involves more intangible elements like brand awareness and perception.

Personalization

Digital marketing allows businesses to personalize their marketing efforts and tailor their messaging to specific target audiences. Traditional marketing tends to be more general and less customizable.

Overall, it's important for businesses to consider both traditional and digital marketing when developing their marketing strategies, as the right mix of tactics can be effective in reaching and engaging with potential customers.

CHAPTER 3

IS THERE ANYTHING LIKE TRADITIONAL & DIGITAL SALES STRATEGIES?

Sales strategies that were effective in the 1980s and 1990s may not be as effective in today's digital-driven age. The rise of the internet and the proliferation of digital technologies have had a significant impact on the way businesses sell their products and services.

In the past, traditional sales strategies such as door-to-door sales, cold calling, and direct mail were commonly used to reach potential customers.

These strategies can still be effective in certain circumstances, but they may not be as effective as they once were due to the rise of digital technologies.

Today, digital sales strategies such as e-commerce, social media selling, and email marketing are becoming more important as consumers increasingly turn to the internet to research and make purchases. These strategies allow businesses to reach and engage with potential customers in a more targeted and personalized way, and they offer a range of tools and technologies for tracking and measuring the effectiveness of sales efforts.

Overall, it's important for businesses to consider both traditional and digital sales strategies when developing their sales plans. The right mix of tactics will depend on the specific needs and goals of the business, as well as the preferences of its target audience. I remember when my mother used to run a small snack business back in 1995. As a child, I would often see her carrying a basket of snacks on her head as she went door-to-door and from family meeting to family meeting, selling her products. It was hard work, but it was also a time when these traditional sales strategies were effective for small businesses.

Fast forward to today, and the landscape has changed significantly. If I were to start a small business today, I would certainly consider using digital sales strategies like WhatsApp messaging to reach and engage with potential customers. With the proliferation of smartphones and messaging platforms, it's easier than ever to connect with people in real-time and offer personalized support and assistance.

Of course, traditional sales strategies can

still be effective in certain circumstances, but it's clear that the digital age has opened up a whole new world of possibilities for businesses looking to sell their products and services. It's important to consider a range of tactics and to choose the strategies that are most effective for reaching and engaging with your target audience.

As a business owner, it's important to stay up -to-date on the latest trends and technologies in order to remain competitive in today's digital landscape. This is especially true when it comes to digital sales strategies.

In the past, traditional sales strategies such as door-to-door sales and in-person meetings were commonly used, but today, digital sales strategies like e-commerce and social media selling are becoming more important as consumers increasingly turn to the internet to research and make purchases.

To be successful in today's business environment, it's critical to upgrade your skills and knowledge in order to effectively implement digital sales strategies. This may involve learning new technologies, staying up-to-date on the latest trends, and developing a deeper understanding of how to effectively reach and engage with potential customers online.

By staying ahead of the curve and adapting to the changing digital landscape, businesses can position themselves for success and engineer strong sales in the digital age. So, it is important for businesses to continuously upgrade their skills and knowledge in order to stay competitive and thrive in the digital world.

CHAPTER 4

DEEP DIVE - TRADITIONAL MARKETING STRATEGIES / SYSTEMS

A) Door-To-Door Marketing

This involves going door-to-door and directly interacting with potential customers to sell products or services.

Here is a step-by-step system for carrying out door-to-door marketing:

Identify Your Target Audience

Determine who you are trying to reach with your door-to-door marketing efforts. This will help you tailor your approach and messaging to the specific needs and interests of your target audience.

Create A List Of Prospects

Develop a list of potential customers to visit by researching demographics, mapping out neighborhoods, and identifying key decision-makers.

Prepare Your Sales Pitch

Practice your sales pitch and make sure you can clearly communicate the benefits of your products or services.

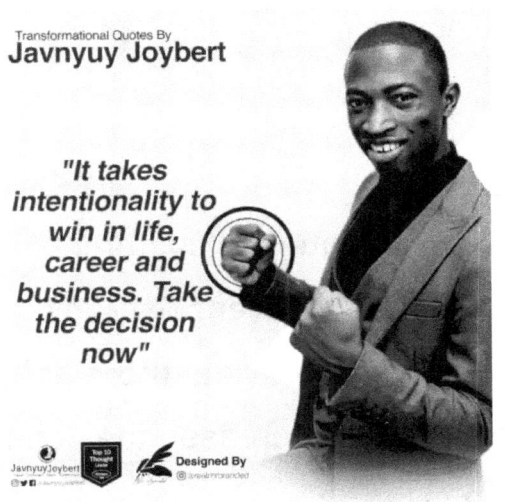

Gather Marketing Materials

Prepare any marketing materials you will need, such as brochures, flyers, or business cards, to give to potential customers.

Knock On Doors

Start knocking on doors and engaging with potential customers in person. Be friendly, polite, and respectful, and be prepared to answer any questions or concerns they may have.

Follow Up

Follow up with potential customers after your initial interaction to answer any additional questions or to provide more information. This can help increase the chances of making a sale.

Evaluate Your Results

Keep track of the results of your door-to-door marketing efforts, including the number of sales made, the response rate, and any feedback you receive. This will help you gauge the effectiveness of your approach and identify areas for improvement.

B) Print Ads

This includes placing ads in newspapers, magazines, and other print media to reach potential customers.

Here is a step-by-step system for creating and placing print ads:

Determine Your Goals

Decide what you want to achieve with your print ad campaign, such as increasing brand awareness, driving traffic to your website, or generating leads.

Identify Your Target Audience

Determine who you are trying to reach with your print ad. This will help you choose the right publication and tailor your messaging to the specific needs and interests of your target audience.

Develop A Creative Concept

Come up with a creative concept for your print ad that will catch the attention of your target audience and effectively communicate your message.

Create The Ad

Design your print ad using graphics, text, and

other visual elements to make it visually appealing and effective.

Place The Ad

Choose the publications in which you want to place your ad, and work with the publication's sales team to determine the best placement and pricing options.

Track Your Results

Keep track of the results of your print ad campaign, including the response rate and any feedback you receive. This will help you gauge the effectiveness of your ad and identify areas for improvement.

Adjust Your Strategy

Based on the results of your print ad campaign, make any necessary adjustments to your strategy to optimize its effectiveness.

C) Radio And Television Commercials

These are audio or video advertisements that are broadcast on radio or television stations.

Radio and television commercials can be a costly marketing strategy for start-ups and small businesses.

However, there are ways for these businesses to get exposure through radio and television without breaking the bank.

One option is to reach out to radio and television shows that have free programs like morning shows or evening shows and request to be a guest.

By establishing a relationship with the hosts and appearing on the show as a guest, businesses can gain exposure to a larger audience without the high cost of creating and airing a commercial.

This strategy may be particularly effective for businesses that are looking to increase brand awareness or generate leads.

Here is a step-by-step system for creating and placing radio and television commercials:

Determine Your Goals

Decide what you want to achieve with your commercial, such as increasing brand awareness, driving traffic to your website, or generating leads.

Identify Your Target Audience

Determine who you are trying to reach with your commercial. This will help you choose the right station and tailor your messaging to the specific needs and interests of your target audience.

Develop A Creative Concept

Come up with a creative concept for your commercial that will catch the attention of your target audience and effectively communicate your message.

Create The Commercial

Write a script, choose a voiceover artist or spokesperson, and produce the commercial using audio and video recording equipment.

Place The Commercial

Work with a media buyer or advertising agency to determine the best radio or television stations and time slots for your commercial.

Track Your Results

Keep track of the results of your commercial campaign, including the response rate and any feedback you receive. This will help you gauge the effectiveness of your commercial and identify areas for improvement.

Adjust Your Strategy

Based on the results of your commercial campaign, make any necessary adjustments to your strategy to optimize its effectiveness. This may involve changing the content of the commercial, the station or time slot in which it is aired, or the frequency of the broadcasts.

Monitor And Maintain Your Campaign

Continue to monitor the results of your commercial campaign and make any necessary adjustments to ensure it is meeting your goals. This may involve rotating the commercial with new creative, targeting different stations or time slots, or adjusting the frequency of the broadcasts.

Overall, it's important to carefully plan and execute your radio and television commercial campaign in order to maximize its effectiveness and reach your desired target audience.

D) Outdoor Advertising

This includes billboards, buses, bus stops, airports, church entrances, school entrances, and other types of outdoor advertisements that are placed in public spaces.

Here is a step-by-step system for creating and placing outdoor advertisements:

Determine Your Goals

Decide what you want to achieve with your outdoor ad campaign, such as increasing brand awareness, driving traffic to your website, or generating leads.

Identify Your Target Audience

Determine who you are trying to reach with your outdoor ad. This will help you choose the right location and tailor your messaging to the specific needs and interests of your target audience.

Develop A Creative Concept

Come up with a creative concept for your outdoor ad that will catch the attention of your target audience and effectively communicate your message.

Create The Ad

Design your outdoor ad using graphics, text, and other visual elements to make it visually appealing and effective.

Place The Ad

Choose the location for your outdoor ad and work with the ad space provider to determine the best placement and pricing options.

Track Your Results

Keep track of the results of your outdoor ad campaign, including the response rate and any feedback you receive. This will help you gauge the effectiveness of your ad and identify areas for improvement.

Adjust Your Strategy

Based on the results of your outdoor ad campaign, make any necessary adjustments to your strategy to optimize its effectiveness. This may involve changing the content of the ad, the location, or the frequency of the ad's display.

Monitor And Maintain Your Campaign

Continue to monitor the results of your outdoor ad campaign and make any necessary adjustments to ensure it is meeting your goals. This may involve rotating the ad with new creative, targeting different locations, or adjusting the frequency of the ad's display.

Overall, it's important to carefully plan and execute your outdoor ad campaign in order to maximize its effectiveness and reach your desired target audience. By choosing the right locations and creating visually appealing and effective ads, businesses can effectively use outdoor advertising as a powerful marketing tool.

E) In-Store Promotions

This includes sales and discounts that are offered in physical stores to attract customers.

Here is a step-by-step system for implementing in-store promotions in a small business:

Determine Your Goals

Decide what you want to achieve with your in-store promotion, such as increasing foot traffic, driving sales, or generating leads.

Identify Your Target Audience

Determine who you are trying to reach with your in-store promotion. This will help you tailor your promotion to the specific needs and interests of your target audience.

Develop A Promotion Strategy

Choose the type of promotion you want to offer, such as a sale, discount, or free gift with purchase. Determine the details of the promotion, such as the duration, terms and conditions, and any exclusions.

Communicate The Promotion

Create marketing materials such as flyers, posters, or social media posts to communicate the promotion to potential customers. Consider using in-store signage and other forms of in-store marketing to draw attention to the promotion.

Implement The Promotion

Implement the promotion in your physical store, ensuring that all employees are aware of the details and can effectively communicate the promotion to customers.

Track Your Results

Keep track of the results of your in-store promotion, including the response rate and any feedback you receive. This will help you gauge the effectiveness of your promotion and identify areas for improvement.

Adjust Your Strategy

Based on the results of your in-store promotion, make any necessary adjustments to your strategy to optimize its effectiveness. This may involve changing the type of promotion offered, the duration of the promotion, or the terms and conditions.

Monitor And Maintain Your Promotion

Continue to monitor the results of your in-store promotion and make any necessary adjustments to ensure it is meeting your goals. This may involve rotating the promotion with new offers or adjusting the terms and conditions.

Overall, it's important to carefully plan and execute your in-store promotion in order to maximize its effectiveness and reach your desired target audience. By offering appealing discounts or sales and effectively communicating the promotion to customers, small businesses can use in-store promotions to drive traffic and sales.

F) Trade Shows And Exhibitions

These events provide an opportunity for businesses to showcase their products and services to a targeted audience.

For this to be successful, the business owner must seek information. Know about small business exhibition and trade shows organized by the chamber of commerce, government agencies and private entities. Follow the process, apply and actively showcase your business. Make sure you build a contact list for further communication. Trade shows and exhibitions are valuable marketing opportunities for businesses to showcase their products and services to a targeted audience.

Here is a step-by-step process for maximizing the benefits of participating in these events:

Research Trade Show And Exhibition Opportunities

Look for events that are relevant to your business and target audience. Consider events organized by chamber of commerce, government agencies, and private entities.

Apply To Participate

Follow the application process for the trade show or exhibition you are interested in participating in. Be sure to carefully review the guidelines and requirements for exhibitors.

Prepare For The Event

Develop a plan for how you will showcase your business at the event, including what products or services you will display, how you will engage with attendees, and any promotional materials you will use.

Build A Contact List

Make sure to collect the contact information of attendees who are interested in your business. This will allow you to follow up with them after the event and continue to nurture relationships.

Actively Participate In The Event

Engage with attendees and make the most of the opportunity to showcase your business. Be sure to follow any guidelines and rules for exhibitors provided by the event organizers.

Follow Up After The Event

Use the contact list you have compiled to follow up with attendees and continue to nurture relationships. This can help generate leads and build your customer base.

Overall, trade shows and exhibitions can be a valuable marketing opportunity for businesses to showcase their products and services and build relationships with potential customers. By carefully planning and actively participating in these events, businesses can maximize the benefits and build their customer base.

G) Public Relations

This involves building relationships with the media and generating positive publicity for a business through press releases, media interviews, and other tactics.

I remember the first time I discovered the power of public relations. I was running my own business and looking for ways to generate positive publicity for my company. That's when I learned about the importance of building relationships with the media.

I started reaching out to media personalities and establishing connections with them. It wasn't always easy, but I knew it was worth the effort. And my hard work paid off. Over the years, I've used public relations tactics like press releases and media interviews to generate a lot of positive publicity for my business.

Personally, I believe that public relations is one of the most effective marketing strategies out there. It's all about building relationships and creating opportunities to share your story with a wider audience. And it's something I've been doing for the past 7 years, with great success.

Step-by-step system for implementing a public relations strategy for your business:

Determine Your Goals

Decide what you want to achieve with your public relations efforts, such as increasing brand awareness, building credibility, or generating leads.

Identify Your Target Audience

Determine who you are trying to reach with your public relations efforts. This will help you tailor your messaging and choose the right media outlets to target.

Develop A PR Plan

Create a plan for how you will build relationships with the media and generate positive publicity for your business. This may include tactics such as crafting press releases, organizing media interviews, or hosting events.

Build Relationships With The Media

Reach out to media outlets and individuals who are relevant to your business and target audience. Establish connections with them and work to build mutually beneficial relationships.

Create Promotional Materials

Develop promotional materials such as press releases, press kits, and media pitches to help communicate your message to the media.

Reach Out To The Media

Use the relationships you have built and the promotional materials you have created to reach out to the media and pitch your story.

Follow Up And Maintain Relationships

Follow up with media outlets and individuals to answer any questions or provide additional information. Continue to nurture these relationships to maintain positive coverage for your business.

Overall, implementing a public relations strategy can be an effective way to generate positive publicity for your business and build relationships with the media. By building relationships, crafting compelling stories, and reaching out to the media, businesses can effectively use public relations to increase brand awareness and

H) Referral Marketing

This involves encouraging satisfied customers to refer their friends and family to a business.

I have found referral marketing to be an incredibly effective marketing strategy for many years. In my training programs, book sales, consulting packages, and even physical product sales, I have consistently seen the power of referral marketing at work.

In fact, I believe that there is no better way to tap into someone's network and leverage their connections than through referral marketing. By consistently delivering high quality products or services and encouraging satisfied customers to refer others, businesses can greatly expand their reach and customer base. I highly recommend incorporating referral marketing into your overall marketing strategy.

Step-by-step process for implementing referral marketing in a small business:

Determine Your Goal

Decide what you want to achieve with your referral marketing efforts, such as increasing customer acquisition, driving sales, or generating leads.

Identify Your Target Audience

Determine who you are trying to reach with your referral marketing efforts. This will help you tailor your strategy and incentives to the specific needs and interests of your target audience.

Develop A Referral Marketing Plan

Create a plan for how you will encourage satisfied customers to refer their friends and family to your business. This may include tactics such as offering incentives or rewards, providing referral tools or materials, or directly asking for referrals.

Foster A Culture Of Referrals

Encourage your team to ask for referrals and make it part of your company culture. This could involve setting goals for referrals or rewarding team members who are successful at generating referrals.

Communicate Your Referral Program

Make sure your customers are aware of your referral program and how they can participate. This may involve creating marketing materials or communicating the program through social media or email.

Track And Measure Your Results

Keep track of the results of your referral marketing efforts, including the number of referrals received and the resulting sales or conversions. This will help you gauge the effectiveness of your program and identify areas for improvement.

Adjust And Optimize Your Strategy

Based on the results of your referral marketing efforts, make any necessary adjustments to your strategy to optimize its effectiveness. This may involve changing the incentives offered, the communication of the program, or the focus of your efforts.

I strongly believe, referral marketing is a powerful way for small businesses to expand their customer base and drive sales.

I) Networking

This involves building relationships with other businesses and individuals in order to generate leads and create opportunities for collaboration.

As a small business owner, I know first-hand how important it is to be strategic with your marketing efforts, especially when you have a limited budget. That's why I believe that building relationships with other businesses and individuals can be one of the most organic and impactful ways to market your business, especially in the start-up or growth phase.

Think about it this way: if you want to ask someone out on a date, you might make friends with their siblings or close friends in order to get to know them better. In the same way, building relationships with other businesses and individuals can help you generate leads and expand your reach.

I've seen this strategy work time and time again in my own business. By being proactive about building relationships and networking with others, I've been able to generate leads and grow my business organically. If you're looking for an effective marketing strategy that won't break the bank, I highly recommend focusing on building relationships with others.

Step-by-step system for implementing networking as a marketing strategy for your business:

Determine Your Goals

Decide what you want to achieve with your networking efforts, such as generating leads, finding new partners or suppliers, or building industry connections.

Identify Your Target Audience

Determine who you want to connect with through networking. This may include other businesses, individuals, or organizations that are relevant to your business and target audience.

Develop A Networking Plan

Create a plan for how you will build relationships with your target audience. This may involve tactics such as attending industry events, joining professional organizations, or participating in online communities.

Build Your Network

Proactively reach out to others and build relationships with them. Be sure to be authentic and genuine in your interactions, and focus on building mutually beneficial connections.

Follow Up And Nurture Relationships

Follow up with the individuals and

businesses you have connected with to continue building relationships and nurture potential opportunities.

Track And Measure Your Results

Keep track of the results of your networking efforts, including the number of leads generated and any opportunities for collaboration that arise.

Adjust And Optimize Your Strategy

Based on the results of your networking efforts, make any necessary adjustments to your strategy to optimize its effectiveness. This may involve changing the tactics you use or the focus of your efforts.

Overall, networking is a powerful way for businesses to generate leads and create opportunities for collaboration. By building relationships with others and nurturing those connections, businesses can expand their reach and grow their business.

CHAPTER 5

DEEP DIVE - DIGITAL MARKETING SYSTEMS / STRATEGIES

A) Content Marketing

Creating and sharing valuable, relevant, and consistent content to attract and retain a clearly defined audience.

I've been a business owner for the past 12 years, and during that time, I've seen first-hand the incredible impact of content marketing. In fact, more than half of my sales can be traced back to content marketing efforts. I truly believe that content marketing is the new gold in the business world.

One of the most powerful things about content marketing is that it helps build credibility for your business. When you consistently create and share valuable, relevant, and consistent content, it helps potential customers see you as an authority in your field and a trusted source of information. This, in turn, can help build trust and make them more likely to see you as the solution to their problems.

So if you're looking for a marketing strategy that can help you build credibility, drive sales, and establish your business as a thought leader, I highly recommend giving content marketing some attention. Trust me, it's worth its weight in gold.

Step-by-step system for implementing content marketing as a strategy for your business:

Determine Your Goals

Decide what you want to achieve with your

content marketing efforts, such as generating leads, driving sales, or increasing brand awareness or building credibility.

Identify Your Target Audience

Determine who you want to reach with your content marketing efforts. This will help you tailor your content to the specific needs, interests of your target audience and also choosing the channel to use.

Develop A Content Marketing Plan

Create a plan for how you will create and share content with your target audience. This may include tactics such as blogging, creating social media posts, or creating video content.

Identify Your Content Types And Distribution Channels

Decide what types of content you will create and how you will share it with your audience. This may include tactics such as email marketing, social media platforms like Facebook, LinkedIn, Instagram, Twitter....

Create And Publish Your Content

Begin creating and publishing your content according to your content marketing plan. Be sure to focus on creating valuable, relevant, and consistent content that resonates with your target audience.

Promote Your Content

Make sure your target audience sees your content by promoting it through your chosen distribution channels. This may include tactics such as social media advertising or email marketing. Sharing on WhatsApp groups and more.

Analyze And Optimize Your Results

Keep track of the results of your content marketing efforts, including metrics such as website traffic, leads generated, and sales. Use this data to identify areas for improvement and optimize your content marketing strategy accordingly.

Content marketing is a powerful way for businesses to attract and retain a clearly defined audience and drive sales. By developing a plan and consistently creating and sharing valuable content, businesses can effectively implement this marketing strategy.

B) Search Engine Optimization (SEO)

Optimize your website and online content to improve your visibility in search engine results pages.

If you want your business to benefit from Search Engine Optimization (SEO), it's important to have a strong website and work with an experienced SEO expert to improve your site's visibility in search engine results pages. A key aspect of SEO is consistently publishing new and relevant content on your website, such as blog posts, news articles, and other information. This helps to keep your site fresh and attract more visitors. In order to effectively implement SEO for your business, it's important to regularly update your website with new content and work with an expert who can help you optimize your site for search engines.

Step-by-step process for implementing search engine optimization (SEO) as a marketing strategy for your business:

Determine Your SEO Goals

Decide what you want to achieve with your SEO efforts, such as increasing website traffic, improving search engine rankings, or generating leads.

Research And Identify Relevant Keywords

Use tools such as keyword research tools or Google's AdWords Keyword Planner to identify the keywords and phrases that are most relevant to your business and target audience. Do not be ignorant about these tools. Or make sure you hire someone who can get this done.

Optimize Your Website

Use the keywords you have identified to optimize your website's content, meta tags, and other elements to improve your visibility in search engine results pages. I suggest you talk to an expert.

Create And Publish High-Quality Content

Consistently create and publish valuable, relevant, and unique content on your website to attract and retain visitors and improve your search engine rankings.

Monitor And Track Your Results

Use tools such as Google Analytics to track the performance of your website and identify areas for improvement.

Continue To Optimize And Update Your Website

Regularly update and optimize your website

to keep it fresh and improve your search engine rankings. This may involve updating your content, adding new pages, or making technical improvements to your site.

SEO is a powerful marketing strategy that can help improve your visibility in search engine results pages and drive more traffic and sales to your business. If you do not have the relevant skills, hire the services of the right professional.

C) Pay-Per-Click (PPC) Advertising

Using online advertising platforms to place sponsored ads on search engine results pages or other websites, and paying a fee each time the ad is clicked.

Step-by-step process for implementing pay-per-click (PPC) advertising as a marketing strategy for your business:

Determine Your PPC Goals

Decide what you want to achieve with your PPC efforts, such as driving website traffic, generating leads, or increasing sales.

Research And Select Your Target Keywords

Use tools such as keyword research tools or Google's AdWords Keyword Planner to identify the keywords and phrases that are most relevant to your business and target audience.

Set Up A PPC Campaign

Use an online advertising platform such as Google Ads to create a PPC campaign and define your target keywords, budget, and other settings.

Create Your Ad Copy And Design Your Ad

Write compelling ad copy and design your ad to attract the attention of your target audience.

Launch Your Campaign

Once your ad is approved, your PPC campaign will go live and your ad will start appearing on search engine results pages or other websites.

Monitor And Optimize Your Campaign

Use tools such as Google Analytics to track the performance of your PPC campaign and identify areas for improvement. Make adjustments to your campaign as needed to optimize your results.

Some examples of platforms for pay-per-click (PPC) advertising include:

Google Ads

The most popular PPC advertising platform, Google Ads, allows businesses to create and place sponsored ads on Google search results pages and other websites that are part of the Google Ads network.

Bing Ads

Another popular PPC advertising platform, Bing Ads allows businesses to create and place sponsored ads on Bing search results pages and other websites that are part of the Bing Ads network.

Facebook Ads

This platform allows businesses to create

and place sponsored ads on the Facebook social media platform, targeting specific demographics and interests.

LinkedIn Ads

LinkedIn Ads allows businesses to create and place sponsored ads on the LinkedIn professional networking platform, targeting specific job titles, industries, and other criteria.

Twitter Ads

This platform allows businesses to create and place sponsored ads on the Twitter social media platform, targeting specific demographics and interests

Instagram Ads

This platform allows businesses to create and place sponsored ads on the Instagram social media platform, targeting specific demographics and interests.

Pinterest Ads

Pinterest Ads allows businesses to create and place sponsored ads on the Pinterest image sharing platform, targeting specific demographics and interests.

Amazon Advertising

This platform allows businesses to create and place sponsored ads on the Amazon e-commerce platform, targeting specific keywords and product categories.

YouTube Ads

This platform allows businesses to create and place sponsored ads on the YouTube video sharing platform, targeting specific demographics and interests.

AdRoll

This is a retargeting platform that allows businesses to create and place sponsored ads on websites and other platforms, targeting users who have previously visited their website or shown interest in their products or services.

D) Email Marketing

Sending targeted, personalized emails to a list of subscribers to nurture leads and drive sales.

I've been using email marketing for my business since 2018, and it has completely transformed my business. One of the things I love about email marketing is the sense of ownership it gives me. When you build an email list of subscribers, you have the ability to reach them anytime you want.

If you create compelling content and establish yourself as an authority and influence among your subscribers, you can reap the rewards. I highly recommend investing in email marketing for any business. It has the potential a gold mine.

Step-by-step process for implementing email marketing as a marketing strategy for your business:

Determine Your Email Marketing Goals

Decide what you want to achieve with your email marketing efforts, such as generating leads, increasing sales, or improving customer retention.

Build Your Email List

Use tactics such as opt-in forms on your website, social media, or in-store to collect email addresses from potential subscribers. Also use gifts like free ebooks or value for people to get when they subscribe.

Suggested platforms you can use for your email marketing: Go to youtube and watch videos on how to use these platforms if you have challenges. Mailchimp (free option), Substack (free) and more.

Create A Email Marketing Plan

Develop a plan for how you will create and send emails to your subscribers, including the types of emails you will send (e.g. newsletters, promotional emails, etc.), how often you will send emails, and what content you will include.

Create Email Templates

Design email templates that you can use for your various types of emails. This will make it easier to create and send emails consistently.

Write And Send Your Emails

Create and send your emails according to your email marketing plan. Be sure to focus on creating targeted, personalized emails that provide value to your subscribers.

Monitor And Track Your Results

Use tools such as email marketing software or Google Analytics to track the performance of your email marketing efforts and identify areas for improvement.

Optimize And Update Your Email Marketing

<u>Strategy</u>

Continuously optimize and update your email marketing strategy based on the results you are seeing. This may involve adjusting your email frequency, testing different subject lines or email designs, or segmenting your email list.

E) Social Media Marketing

Using social media platforms to promote your business, engage with customers, and drive traffic to your website.

We have previously discussed the various ways in which social media platforms can be used. It is clear that being proficient in social media management is crucial for anyone in business, as it will continue to be important in the future. I believe it is essential for anyone in business to not only understand how these platforms work, but also to have a deep understanding of their algorithms. Even if you have hired someone to manage your social media presence, it is still important to master these skills yourself.

Step-by-step process for using social media to promote your business and engage with customers:

Identify Your Target Audience

Determine who your ideal customer is and where they are most likely to be active on social media.

Choose The Right Social Media Platforms

Based on your target audience, select the social media platforms that will be most effective for reaching them.

I typically recommend to my clients that they

focus on a select few social media platforms rather than trying to be active on all of them. This is especially true if they do not have a strong team with the knowledge and skills to create a significant impact on multiple platforms.

Instead, it is more effective to choose the platforms where your target audience is most active. This is why it is important to first identify your target audience and understand their behaviors and preferences.

Some examples of popular social media platforms include:

Facebook

This platform is popular for both personal and business use and allows users to create profiles, connect with friends, and share content.

Twitter

It is a platform is known for its micro blogging format, which allows users to post short updates, or "tweets," of 280 characters or less.

Instagram

This platform is primarily used for sharing photos and videos and is popular among users who want to share their creative content or daily lives.

LinkedIn:

This platform is geared towards professionals and allows users to connect with other professionals in their industry, search for jobs, and showcase their work experience.

TikTok

This platform is known for its short-form videos and is popular among younger users.

Pinterest

This platform is a visual bookmarking tool that allows users to save and discover ideas for their various interests.

YouTube

This platform is a video sharing website that allows users to upload and share their own videos as well as discover and watch videos from others.

Set Up Your Business Profiles

Create profiles for your business on the social media platforms you have selected. Be sure to include all relevant information about your business, such as your website, contact information, and a brief description of your products or services.

Develop A Content Strategy

Plan out the types of content you will post on social media, such as blog posts, images, videos, and promotions.

Create And Schedule Content

Use tools like Hootsuite or Buffer to create and schedule your social media posts in advance.

Engage With Your Audience

Monitor your social media accounts and respond to comments and messages from your followers.

Use Hashtags And Tagging

Use relevant hashtags in your posts to make it easier for people to discover your content. Tag other users and businesses in your posts to increase the visibility of your content.

Use Paid Advertising

Consider using paid advertising on social media to reach a larger audience and drive traffic to your website.

Analyze And Optimize

Use tools like Google Analytics to track the performance of your social media efforts and identify areas for improvement.

F) Influencer Marketing

Partnering with influencers or industry experts to promote your business and reach a larger audience.

Influencer marketing involves partnering with individuals who have a large following on social media, or who are considered experts in a particular industry, to promote your business to their audience. These individuals, known as influencers, have the ability to reach a large number of people and can potentially help to increase brand awareness and drive sales for your business.

To partner with an influencer, you would typically negotiate a deal in which the influencer promotes your business or product in exchange for a fee or other compensation. This promotion can take the form of sponsored posts, product reviews, or other forms of content.

Influencer marketing can be an effective way to reach a larger audience and can be especially useful for businesses that are trying to reach a younger, more digitally-savvy demographic. However, it is important to carefully research and select influencers who align with your brand values and whose audience is relevant to your business.

G) Video Marketing

Creating and sharing video content to promote your business and engage with customers.

We are in the age of video marketing. Video marketing is more important now than ever before. From short to long videos, creating engaging and captivating video content is a crucial element of any successful marketing strategy in today's digital age.

By creating and sharing video content, you can effectively promote your business, engage with customers, and stand out in a crowded online marketplace. Don't miss out on the opportunity to leverage the power of video marketing – start creating and sharing video content to give your business the boost it needs.

As an entrepreneur, I understand the importance of constantly learning and improving my skills in order to stay competitive in the marketplace. That's why I was determined to develop my videography skills, even though I didn't have any formal training or access to expensive equipment.

I started by experimenting with different apps and software programs, learning how to use them to create and edit basic videos. It wasn't always easy – there were plenty of challenges and setbacks along the way – but I was determined to succeed. And as it turns out, all of that hard work paid off.

Today, I use my videography skills on a

regular basis to promote my business and engage with customers. And even though I still use my phone to record and simple apps to edit, I've been able to create professional-quality videos that have helped me stand out in a crowded marketplace.

So if you're an entrepreneur who's been avoiding video marketing because you don't think you have the necessary skills or resources, I encourage you to give it a try. With a little bit of practice and determination, you too can learn the skills and make things happen.

H) Mobile Marketing

Using mobile apps, SMS, and other mobile channels to reach customers and promote your business.

Mobile marketing refers to the use of mobile apps, SMS (short message service), and other mobile channels to reach and engage with customers for the purpose of promoting your business. It is an effective way to reach a large audience, as the majority of people now access the internet and social media through their smartphones.

There are many different ways to use mobile marketing to promote your business. For example, you could create a mobile app for your business and use push notifications to send updates, promotions, and other information to your customers. You could also use SMS messaging to send coupons, discounts, or other offers to your customers. Additionally, you could use mobile advertising to reach customers on popular apps and websites.

Overall, mobile marketing is a powerful tool for reaching and engaging with customers in today's digital world. By utilizing mobile channels to promote your business, you can effectively reach a large audience and drive sales and engagement.

Here are some examples of mobile marketing strategies that businesses might use:

Creating A Mobile App

Businesses can create their own mobile app, which can be downloaded by users and used to access information about the business, make purchases, or receive updates and promotions.

SMS Messaging

Businesses can use SMS messaging to send

coupons, discounts, or other offers to customers who have opted-in to receive them.

Mobile Advertising

Businesses can use mobile advertising to reach customers on popular apps and websites. This can include banner ads, interstitial ads, or native ads that are integrated into the content of an app or website.

Mobile-Optimized Emails

Businesses can use mobile-optimized emails to reach customers through their smartphones. These emails are designed to be easily readable on a small screen and may include links to mobile-optimized web pages or other resources.

QR Codes

Businesses can use QR codes, which can be scanned with a smartphone camera, to provide customers with access to information or special offers.

WhatsApp

WhatsApp is a popular messaging app that can be used as a mobile marketing tool. WhatsApp allows users to create status updates, groups, and broadcast lists, which can be used to reach and engage with customers in a number of ways.

For example, a business could use a WhatsApp status update to share a promotional message or announcement with their customers. They could create a WhatsApp group for their customers to join, which could be used to share updates, offer support, or facilitate discussions. They could also use a WhatsApp broadcast list to send messages to a large number of people at once.

Overall, WhatsApp can be a useful mobile marketing tool for businesses that want to reach and engage with their customers through this popular messaging app.

By using these and other mobile marketing strategies, businesses can effectively reach and engage with their customers through their smartphones.

I) Affiliate Marketing

Partnering with other individuals and businesses to promote your products or services and earning a commission for each sale made.

Affiliate marketing is a performance-based marketing strategy in which businesses partner with individuals or other businesses (called affiliates) to promote their products or services. In exchange for promoting the business's products or services, affiliates earn a commission for each sale that they help to generate.

Affiliate marketing can be an effective way for businesses to reach a larger audience and drive sales. It can also be a lucrative opportunity for affiliates, who can earn a commission for promoting products or services that they believe in.

To participate in affiliate marketing, businesses create a program for affiliates to join. The business provides affiliates with unique tracking links, codes or other resources that they can use to promote the business's products or services. When a customer clicks on one of these links and makes a purchase, the affiliate earns a commission.

Step-by-step process for implementing an affiliate marketing program:

Determine Your Goals

Before you begin, it is important to determine what you hope to achieve with your affiliate marketing program. Do you want to increase brand awareness, drive traffic to your website, or boost sales? Clearly defining your goals will help you to focus your efforts and measure the success of your program.

Set Up Your Affiliate Program

Once you have chosen an affiliate network, you will need to set up your affiliate program by creating a program description and terms and conditions. You will also need to decide on the commission structure and any other incentives that you will offer to affiliates.

Recruit Affiliates

Next, you will need to recruit affiliates to join your program. You can do this through your own marketing efforts or by using the resources provided by the affiliate network.

Provide Resources To Affiliates

Once you have recruited affiliates, it is important to provide them with the resources they need to promote your products or services effectively. This may include banner ads, product images, and other promotional materials.

Monitor And Track Results

Use the tracking and reporting tools provided by the affiliate network to monitor the performance of your affiliate program. This will help you to identify which affiliates are performing well and to make any necessary adjustments to your program.

J) Display Advertising

Using online advertising platforms to place banner ads or other display ads on websites or social media platforms to reach a targeted audience.

Display advertising refers to the use of online advertising platforms to place banner ads or other types of display ads on websites or social media platforms. These ads are designed to reach a targeted audience and can be used to promote a business, product, or service.

There are many different online advertising

platforms that businesses can use to place display ads. These platforms allow businesses to create and target ads based on specific criteria, such as location, demographics, interests, and behaviors. Once the ad is created and the target audience is defined, the platform will automatically place the ad on websites or social media platforms that are visited by the target audience.

Display advertising can be an effective way for businesses to reach a targeted audience and drive traffic to their website or other online properties. It can also be used to retarget website visitors who have shown an interest in the business, by displaying ads to them as they visit other websites or social media platforms.

One way to utilize display advertising is by working with bloggers who run high-traffic blogs. These bloggers can display your advertising banners on the homepage of their blogs, as well as on popular posts, for a specified period of time. In exchange, you pay a fee. This can be an effective way to reach a targeted audience and promote your business to a large number of people.

K) Retargeting

Using cookies or other tracking technologies to show targeted ads to users who have visited your website or engaged with your business in some way.

This particular strategy is very powerful and works magic.

Retargeting is a way to show ads to people who have already visited your website or who have shown an interest in your business in some way. It works by using cookies or other tracking technologies to remember which websites people have visited. Then, when those people visit other websites or social media platforms, they might see ads for your business.

For example, let's say a person visits your website to learn more about your company. They might look at different pages and learn about your products or services. Later, when they are browsing other websites or social media platforms, they might see ads for your business. These ads might remind them about your company and encourage them to visit your website again or make a purchase. Retargeting can be a helpful way to keep your business top of mind with people who are interested in what you have to offer. If you own a business and want to try retargeting, you can use tools like Google AdWords or Facebook Ads to create and display ads to people who have visited your website.

L) Personalization

Using data and analytics to deliver personalized and targeted marketing messages to individual customers or segments of customers.

This works especially when you are selling expensive or premium services and products. Personalization is a way to make marketing messages feel more special and relevant to each person who sees them. It works by using data and analytics to understand what people like and what they are interested in. Then, businesses can use that information to create marketing messages that are tailored specifically to each person or group of people.

For example, let's say a person buys a toy car from a toy store. The store might use personalization to send that person an email thanking them for their purchase and suggesting other toy cars that they might like based on their previous purchase. The email might also include a special discount or promotion that is only available to that person.

Personalization can be a helpful way to make marketing messages feel more special and to encourage people to make more purchases. If you own a business and want to try personalization, you can use tools like email marketing software or customer relationship management (CRM) software to create and send personalized marketing messages to your customers.

M) Chatbots

Using artificial intelligence and machine learning to create automated chatbots that can interact with customers and provide information or assistance.

Chatbots are computer programs that can automatically respond to messages and perform tasks. They are used by a variety of businesses, from small to large, to assist with customer service and other tasks. For example, you might have seen chatbots on WhatsApp Business automatically replying to certain messages, or on Facebook pages responding to customer inquiries. Even banks use chatbots to provide customer service.

To use a chatbot for your business, you will need to hire someone with the skills to build the chatbot for you. This person will work with you to understand the needs of your business and design a chatbot that can help you to interact with customers, answer their questions, and perform other tasks. Once the chatbot is built, you can use it to help manage your business and improve customer satisfaction.

Chatbots can be an effective tool for marketing and sales conversion. They can help to generate leads, which are potential customers who have expressed an interest in your business, and manage those leads in order to increase the chances of conversion. For example, a chatbot might interact with a potential customer, gather information about their needs and interests, and then provide them with information about your products or services that are most relevant to them. This can help to nurture the lead and increase the chances of a successful sale. Overall, chatbots can be a valuable asset for businesses that want to improve their marketing and sales efforts

N) Interactive Content

Creating content such as quizzes, polls, or surveys that engage users and encourage them to interact with your business.

Interactive content is a type of content that is designed to engage users and encourage them to interact with your business. It can take many different forms, such as quizzes, polls, surveys, or games. The goal of interactive content is to create a more immersive and engaging experience for users, which can help to build brand loyalty and drive business objectives.

For example, a business might create a quiz about a particular product or service that asks users to answer questions and provides them with personalized results. This can be an effective way to educate users about the product and generate leads by gathering information about their interests and needs. A poll or survey can be used to gather feedback from users and understand their preferences and opinions. And a game can be a fun way to engage users and promote a business or product.

Overall, interactive content can be a powerful tool for engaging users and encouraging them to interact with your business. By creating and sharing this type of content, you can build a more meaningful connection with your audience and drive business objectives.

Step-by-step process for implementing interactive content in a small business:

Determine Your Goals

Before you begin, it is important to determine what you hope to achieve with your interactive content. Do you want to increase brand awareness, gather feedback from users, or generate leads? Clearly defining your goals will help you to focus your efforts and measure the success of your content.

Choose The Type Of Interactive Content

There are many different types of interactive content that you can create, including quizzes, polls, surveys, and games. Consider your business goals and the interests of your audience when selecting the type of content that you will create.

Create The Content

Use a tool or platform to create your

interactive content. This might include designing the layout, writing the questions or prompts, and adding any necessary images or graphics.

Promote The Content

Once your interactive content is created, it is important to promote it to your audience. You can do this through social media, email marketing, or other channels.

On social media platform, it can be as simple as asking a question and requesting followers to give their responses in the comment section and you follow carefully to gather the relevant data, direct them to your website or a link to read more and buy your product or service.

Analyze The Results

Use the analytics and reporting tools provided by the platform or tool you used to create your interactive content to track the performance of your content. This will help you to understand how well it is resonating with your audience and to identify any areas for improvement.

O) Virtual Events

Hosting virtual events such as webinars or live streams to connect with customers and promote your business.

Virtual events can be an extremely effective way to launch a new product or service, particularly if it is innovative or a premium offering. I have personally used virtual events countless times to launch new products and services, and have always seen great results.

Not only do virtual events allow you to reach a large and diverse audience, but they also provide an opportunity to showcase your product or service in a professional and engaging way. If you are looking to launch a new product or service, I highly recommend hosting a virtual event. It can be a powerful tool for promoting your business and generating buzz around your offering.

Virtual events are online events that are hosted via the internet, such as webinars or live streams. They provide a way for businesses to connect with customers and promote their products or services in a virtual setting.

Webinars are a type of virtual event that typically involve a presentation or lecture given by an expert on a particular topic. They can be live or pre-recorded, and are often interactive, allowing attendees to ask questions or participate in discussions.

Live streams are similar to webinars, but they are usually more informal and unscripted. They may involve a live Q&A session, a product demo, or other interactive activities.

Virtual events can be an effective way for businesses to reach a large audience, even if they are not able to meet in person. They provide an opportunity to engage with customers, showcase products or services, and build brand awareness. If you are new to this and want to learn more about virtual events, you can consider attending webinars or live streams hosted by businesses or organizations in your field of study.

Virtual events can be hosted on platforms like Facebook live, LinkedIn live, Zoom, Streamyard, Instagram live and more.

P) Customer Reviews And Ratings

Encouraging customers to leave reviews or ratings on your website or social media platforms, and using those reviews to improve your business and build trust with potential customers.

As an entrepreneur, it is important to actively seek out customer reviews and ratings. These can be powerful marketing and sales tools that can help you to attract new customers and build credibility for your business.

Whenever a customer tells you that they had a great experience with your service, be sure to direct them to a place where they can leave a positive review for others to see. This could be a review website, social media platform, or your own website. By encouraging your customers to leave reviews and ratings, you can build a reputation for providing excellent service and help to grow your business.

Customer reviews and ratings are written or numerical evaluations that customers leave about their experiences with your business. These evaluations can be positive, negative, or neutral, and they are often shared on the business's website or social media platforms. As a business owner, it is important to encourage your customers to leave reviews and ratings about their experiences with your company. These evaluations can provide valuable insights into what is working well and what could be improved, and they can also help to build trust with potential customers.

When people are considering making a purchase from a business, they often look for reviews and ratings to help them make an informed decision. By having a large number of positive reviews and ratings, you can show potential customers that your business is trustworthy and that others have had positive experiences with it.

To encourage your customers to leave reviews and ratings, you can ask them for feedback directly or provide links to review websites or social media platforms where they can leave their evaluations. You can also use email marketing or other channels to remind customers to leave reviews or ratings. By actively seeking out and using customer reviews and ratings, you can improve your business and build trust with potential customers.

Q) User-Generated Content

Encouraging customers to share photos,

videos, or other content featuring your products or services, and using that content to promote your business.

Let me share with you an amazing story.

One day, a clever business owner had an idea to encourage her customers to take selfies in restaurant. She knew that if they shared these selfies on their personal social media platforms and tagged her business, it could be a powerful way to market her company and even drive sales.

So, she put up signs around her store and included cards with each purchase that asked customers to snap a selfie and share their positive feedback on their social media accounts. The customers loved the idea and happily obliged.

As the selfies started rolling in, the business

owner was amazed at the response. People were sharing their selfies and tagging her business left and right, and she started to see a surge in traffic and sales. It was clear that this fun and interactive marketing strategy was working like a charm.

From that day on, the business owner knew that encouraging her customers to take selfies and share their positive experiences on social media was one of the most powerful ways to market her business and drive sales. And the best part was, it was easy and enjoyable for everyone involved.

User-generated content is any type of content that is created and shared by customers or users of a business's products or services. This content can take many forms, such as photos, videos, reviews, or testimonials, and it is often shared on social media or other online platforms.

By encouraging your customers to create and share user-generated content, you can promote your business in a more authentic and engaging way. This type of content is often more trusted and influential than traditional advertising, as it comes from real people who have firsthand experience with your products or services. By using user-generated content to promote your business, you can build credibility, trust, and brand loyalty with your customers.

CHAPTER 6

DEEP DIVE - SALES STRATEGIES

After implementing effective traditional and digital marketing strategies, it is crucial to design and implement effective sales strategies in order to convert leads into paying customers. Without these strategies, your marketing efforts may be in vain as you will be unable to turn potential customers into paying ones.

It is important to have a clear plan in place for converting leads, as this will help you to maximize the return on your marketing investments and drive business growth.

To consistently drive sales growth in your business, it is important to master a few key sales strategies and challenge your sales team to excel in these areas. These strategies can help you to convert leads into paying customers and drive business growth. It is critical to intentionally focus on mastering these strategies and to encourage your sales team to do the same in order to achieve the best possible results.

Let us break down the sales strategies and how to implement them immediately. Let's go;

A) Offering Incentives

This could include discounts, free gifts, or other perks that are designed to encourage leads to make a purchase.

Offering incentives is a sales strategy that involves providing customers with discounts, free gifts, or other perks in order to encourage them to make a purchase. The goal of this strategy is to create value for customers and motivate them to take action.

For example, a business might offer a discount to customers who make a purchase within a certain timeframe like during Easter Season, Christmas, new year, business anniversary, or a free gift with a purchase of a certain amount. These incentives can be effective at encouraging leads to make a purchase, particularly if they feel that they are getting a good deal or added value.

Incentives can be used in a variety of ways, such as through email marketing campaigns, social media promotions, or in-store displays. By offering incentives to leads, you can create motivation for them to take action and make a purchase. This can be a powerful way to drive sales and increase customer loyalty.

B) Providing Excellent Customer Service

By offering timely and helpful support to leads, you can increase their likelihood of making a purchase.

Providing excellent customer service is a powerful sales conversion strategy that can not only convert a particular customer, but also influence them to refer your business to their network. It is important to prioritize customer service and not to take it lightly, as it can have a significant impact on the success of your business.

By consistently providing high-quality service to your customers, you can create a positive experience for them and increase the likelihood of converting them into paying customers. Additionally, satisfied customers are more likely to refer your business to others, which can help you to grow your customer base and drive sales.

Asking for the sale: This might seem obvious, but sometimes simply asking leads to make a purchase can be effective. You can do this through email marketing, follow-up calls, or other channels.

Step-by-step process for implementing excellent customer service in your business:

Determine Your Customer Service Goals

Before you begin, it is important to define what you hope to achieve with your customer service efforts. Do you want to increase customer satisfaction, reduce churn, or drive sales? Clearly defining your goals will help you to focus your efforts and measure the success of your customer service efforts.

Train Yourself And Your Team

Make sure that your customer service team is well-trained and equipped to handle customer inquiries and concerns. This might include training on your products or services, communication skills, and problem-solving techniques.

Establish A Customer Service Process

Develop a clear process for handling customer inquiries and concerns, including how to escalate issues and resolve problems. Make sure that your team understands this process and is able to follow it consistently.

Monitor And Measure Your Performance

Use customer feedback and metrics such as

response time and resolution rate to track your customer service performance. This will help you to identify areas for improvement and adjust your efforts as needed.

Continuously Improve

Look for ways to continuously improve your customer service efforts. This might include implementing new technologies, gathering customer feedback, or making changes to your process.

C) Creating A Sense Of Urgency

By highlighting limited time offers or other reasons why leads should act now, you can increase the likelihood of a sale.

Let me show you how this works best with this business story.

There was a small business owner who wanted to increase sales, but she wasn't having much luck. She decided to try a new strategy: creating a sense of urgency.

She started by highlighting limited time offers on her website and social media channels. She made it clear that these deals would only be available for a short time, and encouraged customers to act quickly in order to take advantage of them.

To her surprise, the strategy worked like a charm. Customers started responding to the limited time offers and making purchases at a faster rate. The business owner was thrilled with the results and continued to use this strategy on a regular basis.

As she saw her sales increase, the business owner realized the power of creating a sense of urgency. By highlighting limited time offers and other reasons why customers should act now, she was able to increase the likelihood of making a sale. And as her business grew, she knew that this strategy had played a critical role in her success.

Step-by-step process for implementing a sense of urgency in your sales efforts:

Determine What Will Create A Sense Of Urgency For Your Customers

This might be a limited time offer, a shortage of a popular product, or a special sale event. Consider what will motivate your customers to take action and make a purchase.

Communicate The Sense Of Urgency To Your Leads

Once you have identified what will create a sense of urgency, make sure to communicate this effectively to your leads. Use email marketing, social media, or other channels to highlight the limited time offer or other reason for acting now.

Create A Sense Of Exclusivity

Make your leads feel special by offering them something that is not available to everyone. This could be a VIP discount or early access to a new product.

Use Scarcity To Your Advantage

If you have a limited supply of a product or service, make sure to communicate this to your leads. This can create a sense of urgency and motivate them to take action.

Follow Up With Leads Who Have Not Acted

If you have leads who have not yet made a purchase, consider following up with them to remind them of the limited time offer or other reason to act now. This can help to create a sense of urgency and increase the likelihood of a sale.

D) Offering multiple purchase options

By providing a range of purchasing options, such as different pricing tiers or financing options, you can make it easier for leads to make a purchase.

People enjoy having choices and the ability to make their own decisions. Providing multiple purchase options to customers can have a strong psychological effect, as it allows them to feel a sense of control. This can ultimately lead to increased sales.

Offering multiple purchase options allows customers to choose the option that best fits their budget or preferences. For example, if you are selling a product, you could offer different pricing tiers (options) based on the features included or the quantity of the product being purchased. This can help to appeal to a wider range of customers, as some may be willing to pay more for additional features or a larger quantity, while others may be looking for a more affordable option.

Additionally, offering financing options, such as a payment plan or the ability to pay with a credit card, mobile money, can make it easier for leads to make a purchase, as they may not have to pay the full amount upfront. By providing multiple purchasing options, you can increase the chances of making a sale and make the purchasing process more convenient for the customer.

Here is an example of how a small business

could practice offering multiple purchase options: We will use the dollar currency to fit all nations.

Let's say you own a small bakery and you sell homemade cakes. One way you could offer multiple purchase options is by providing different sizes of cakes at different price points. For example, you could offer a small cake for $20, a medium cake for $30, and a large cake for $40. This allows customers to choose the size that best fits their needs and budget. You could also offer additional options such as different flavors or the ability to customize the cake with a message or specific design.

Another way you could practice offering multiple purchase options is by offering financing options for your cakes. For example, you could allow customers to pay with a credit card or offer a payment plan for larger purchases. This can make it easier for customers to make a purchase, as they may not have to pay the full amount upfront.

By offering these types of purchasing options, you can make it easier for leads to make a purchase and increase the chances of making a sale.

Step by step process for implementing the practice of offering multiple purchase options:

Identify The Options You Can Offer

The first step is to consider the different options you can offer to customers. This could include different pricing options like in the example above, financing options, customization options, or other types of choices.

Think about what would be most appealing to your target audience and how these options can add value for the customer.

Determine The Cost And Feasibility Of Each Option

Once you have identified the options you can offer, the next step is to determine the cost and feasibility of each option. This will help you to understand how these options will impact your business and ensure that you can offer them in a way that is financially sustainable and will fit your target market.

Communicate The Options To Customers

After you have determined which options you can offer and how they will be implemented, the next step is to communicate these options to customers. This can be done through your website, product listings, marketing materials, or in-person interactions with customers.

Implement The Options

The final step is to put the options into practice. This may involve updating your website or product listings, setting up financing options, or making any other necessary changes to allow customers to take advantage of the options you are offering.

By following these steps, you can effectively implement the practice of offering multiple purchase options and make it easier for leads to make a purchase.

E) Making Sales Presentations To Influence Customers To Make The

Buying Decision

The ability to effectively deliver a sales presentation, whether using a PowerPoint or not, is essential for driving sales. Strong presentation skills are critical for businesses seeking to increase their sales.

There are various ways in which businesses can conduct sales presentations, including one-on-one with a customer, to a group of customers, in a seminar or conference, or through an online webinar on platforms such as Zoom, Facebook, LinkedIn, or Instagram. Organizing an information session or large conference can also be an effective way to present to a larger audience and drive sales.

Sales presentations are a way for businesses to communicate the benefits and value of their products or services to potential customers in an effort to influence them to make a purchase. A well-crafted sales presentation can persuade the customer to see the value in what is being offered and make the decision to buy.

There are several components that can make a sales presentation effective at influencing the customer's buying decision. These include:

Identifying The Customer's Needs

Understanding the customer's needs and pain points can help you tailor the presentation to address their specific concerns and show how your product or service can solve their problems.

Providing Evidence Of The Product Or Service's Value

Use data, customer testimonials, and other evidence to demonstrate the value of your product or service. This can help to build trust and credibility with the customer.

Addressing Objections

Anticipate and address any potential objections or concerns the customer may have. This can help to build confidence in the product or service and overcome any hesitation the customer may have about making a purchase.

Closing The Sale

End the presentation with a clear call to action, such as asking the customer to make a purchase or schedule a follow-up meeting to discuss the next steps.

By following these steps, a sales presentation can be an effective way to influence customers to make the buying decision.

CHAPTER 7

CLOSING DEALS

(If You Cannot Close Deals, Your Business Will Die Soon)

Closing sales deals, or persuading customers to make a purchase, is a critical aspect of running a business. If a business is unable to close sales deals, it will not generate revenue and will ultimately struggle to survive.

Every successful business has individuals or teams who have mastered the art and science of closing deals. These individuals ensure that all leads generated through marketing efforts are converted into paying customers through a well-executed closing process.

In other words, the ability to close deals is a crucial component of business success.

Closing deals, or persuading customers to make a purchase, is a critical aspect of running a business. Without the ability to close deals, a business will not generate revenue and will ultimately struggle to survive. Therefore, it is important for businesses to have dedicated individuals or teams who are skilled at closing deals and can effectively convert leads into paying customers.

Step by step process for closing a deal with a customer after they have expressed interest in your product or service:

Confirm The Customer's Needs

Make sure you understand the customer's needs and the specific problems they are trying to solve with your product or service.

Review The Benefits And Features Of Your Product Or Service

Highlight the key benefits and features of your product or service and how they meet the customer's needs.

Address Any Objections

Anticipate and address any potential objections or concerns the customer may have. This can help to build confidence in your product or service and overcome any hesitation the customer may have about making a purchase.

Make The Offer

Present a clear and compelling offer, including the price and any special promotions or incentives you are offering.

Close The Sale

End the conversation with a clear call to action, such as asking the customer to make a purchase or schedule a follow-up meeting to discuss the next steps.

It is essential for the salesperson or businessperson to have confidence, charisma, and a thorough understanding of the product in order to successfully close a deal. Poor communication or a lack of knowledge about the product can hinder the ability to close the sale. Therefore, it is important to be well-prepared and confident when engaging with customers in order to increase the chances of closing a deal.

Go through this sample discussion between a customer and a sales person. It is for the purpose of learning:

Salesperson: Hi [customer], it's great to meet you. I understand you're interested in our [product]. Can you tell me a bit more about the challenges you're hoping to solve with this product?

Customer: Yes, we're looking for a solution to [problem] and we think your product might be able to help.

Salesperson: Absolutely. Our [product] is specifically designed to solve [problem] and has helped many of our customers achieve great results. In fact, [insert customer testimonial or case study].

Customer: That's really impressive. Can you tell me more about the features of the product and how it works?

Salesperson: Of course. [Product] has [list key features] and is very easy to use. Simply [explain how the product works].

Customer: That sounds great. How much does it cost?

Salesperson: The retail price for [product] is [price], but I'm able to offer you a special promotion today of [discounted price]. This promotion includes [list any additional perks or incentives].

Customer: Wow, that's a great deal. Can I think about it and get back to you?

Salesperson: Absolutely. I understand that making a purchasing decision can take some time. However, I want to let you know that this promotion is only available for a limited time. If you're interested in taking advantage of this offer, I recommend making a decision soon.

Customer: Okay, I'll let you know by

tomorrow.

Salesperson: Great, I'll look forward to hearing from you. In the meantime, if you have any additional questions or concerns, don't hesitate to reach out. Thank you for considering our product.

<u>CONCLUSION</u>

If you have read this book, *Skyrocket Your Profits: 25 Marketing & Sales Proven Strategies to Boost Your Sales*, up until this point, you are likely armed with a range of strategies to implement in your business.

However, it's important to note that simply having these strategies is not enough. In order to truly see success in your business, you must be willing to put in the hard work and consistently apply these strategies.

Remember, relevant strategies in the hands of a lazy person are useless. **Don't let the hope of success be overshadowed by a lack of action**. Take charge of your business and start implementing these strategies today.

With dedication and hard work, you can transform your business and achieve the success you desire. Don't forget to share your success stories with me.